SPRING

John Schlageck, Kansas Farm Bureau

Ken Kashian, Illiniois Farm Bureau

SUMMER

Ken Kashian, Illinois Farm Bureau

FALL

WINTER

THE SEASONS OF
FARM BUREAU

EDITED BY MACE THORNTON

PUBLISHED BY THE AMERICAN FARM BUREAU RESEARCH FOUNDATION

THE AMERICAN FARM BUREAU RESEARCH FOUNDATION

By ensuring funds are available to conduct essential agricultural research, farmers and ranchers can secure the future of agriculture. "Securing our Future" is the ongoing theme of the American Farm Bureau Research Foundation — an organization founded and run by agricultural producers for the betterment of the industry.

The American Farm Bureau Research Foundation was founded in 1967 by the American Farm Bureau Federation for the purposes of initiating and financing agricultural research and education activities. The Foundation is classified as a charitable organization under Section 501(c)(3) of the Internal Revenue Service Code.

The Foundation is funded by contributions from individuals, county and state Farm Bureaus and through financial support from corporations and other foundations. An endowment fund has been established to provide support for projects in the future. Your donation, as commemorated by this book, is an essential part of making agriculture's future secure.

For more information, contact: American Farm Bureau Research Foundation, 225 Touhy Avenue, Park Ridge, IL 60068. Phone:(312) 399-5764.

Special thanks are extended to all who contributed photographs and essays, to Elizabeth Bodo and Jack King for their support and assistance, and to the American Farm Bureau Research Foundation Board of Directors for making this book possible.

Editor: Mace Thornton
Associate Editor: Marsha Purcell
Executive Editor: William Strode
Production Manager: Doug Bartholomew
Contributing Editors: Christopher Noun and Nancy Swanson
Library of Congress Catalog Number: 93-80190
Hardcover International Standard Book Number 1-56469-018-0
First Edition printed Fall, 1993 by Harmony House Publishers,
Book designed and produced by Harmony House Publishers,
P. O. Box 90, Prospect, Kentucky 40059 (502) 228-2010 / 228-4446
Copyright © 1993 by American Farm Bureau Research Foundation
Photographs contributed by State Farm Bureaus and other agencies
Cover photograph by Ken Kashian, Illnois Farm Bureau
Printed in Canada

CONTENTS

American Farm Bureau Federation General Offices, Park Ridge, Ill.   *Nancy Swanson, American Farm Bureau Federation*

FOREWORD: THE SEASONS OF FARM BUREAU

By Mace Thornton
American Farm Bureau Federation

"To every thing there is a season, and a time to every purpose under the heaven. A time to be born, and a time to die. A time to plant and a time to pluck up that which was planted."
Ecclesiastes 2:16

Of all the natural cycles that give order to earthly chaos, none claim more influence over agriculture than the four seasons. Fall, winter, spring and summer each present unique travails and tributes. Year after year, America's farmers and ranchers abide by these eternal truths while producing food and fiber for the world.

Though the formal definition of "season" is bound by the year's equinoctial spans, to farmers and ranchers it denotes other less formal durations — planting season, harvest season, calving season, grazing season . . . While these agrarian "seasons" spill across casual boundaries, their ceremonies are self-defining.

Regional rituals, such as "putting up" the first cutting of Oregon alfalfa and "wet harvesting" New England cranberry bogs, commemorate the year's ripening with unrivaled precision.

As an organization whose members grow every farm commodity produced in the nation, Farm Bureau is active in all seasons, but its annual timetable is set in deference to the sun's equatorial passings and the related tasks nature assigns its members.

Just as a year would not be complete without Louisiana farmers piloting boats through flooded rice fields to gather crawfish, or Kentucky farmers ascending the steps of the nation's Capitol to visit lawmakers, nor would the year be whole without the quintessential Farm Bureau annual meeting.

The following essays and photographs, gleaned from more than 1,000 submissions, represent agriculture in the 50 states and Puerto Rico. This bound volume, through photographer's lens and writer's prose, chronicles Farm Bureau, its members and their pursuits during spring, summer, fall and winter — "The Seasons of Farm Bureau."

Farmer Keith Fowler. *Pettus Read, Tennessee Farm Bureau Federation*

SPRING

"In our springtime every day has its hidden growth in the mind,
as it has in the earth
when the little folded blades are getting ready to pierce the ground."

George Eliot (Marion Evans Cross)

Proper planning is part of the job. *Maryland Farm Bureau*

Diane and Chuck Souther use integrated pest management in their New Hampshire orchard.
Joan Waldoch, American Farm Bureau Federation

Louisiana Young Farmer of the Year award recipients Jennifer and Nolan Clark. *Felton Vickers, Louisiana Farm Bureau Federation*

Iverson tulips paint the landscape. *Rick Stevenson, Oregon Farm Bureau Federation*

Following page: Rick Stevenson, Oregon Farm Bureau Federation

TWENTY ACRES OF LIVING COLOR

By Rick Stevenson
Oregon Farm Bureau Federation

Color awaits the spring sightseer who travels down Newman Road near Mt. Angel, Oregon. This vibrant color signals the passing of winter and the coming of spring. Twenty acres of tulips become a showcase for the changing season on the Iverson family farm in Oregon's mid-Willamette Valley.

Ross and Dorothy Iverson, along with sons Steve, Nels, Ken, and Paul, and daughters Karen and Barb, make up a savvy and diversified farming operation that grows chipping potatoes, row crops, nursery crops, and tulips. The daughters and daughters-in-law, Denise, Patti, Vicki, and Janet, make up the Wooden Shoe Bulb Company — the retail side of the family tulip business.

The Iversons' nurturing handiwork culminates with their spring tulip show in late March and early April. They have hosted thousands of people at their tulip fields, where visitors can view 150 varieties of tulips. The farm offers fresh-cut tulips and daffodils and the chance to order bulbs through their catalog. The Iversons' market extends well beyond the field, with shipments of cut flowers traveling to all parts of the country.

As cars and tour buses pull into the field and view the rainbow of colors framed against the Cascade Mountains and majestic Mt. Hood, workers go about the field picking flowers.

Closed tulips are picked carefully for the wholesale florist market to ensure that buds are not damaged. The pickers are trained to pick the tight buds, and stems are snapped off above the base leaf — no clipper can be used so as not to spread disease.

The flowers are bunched in groups of 10 stems of the same variety and gathered quickly for transporting to the processing shed. A crew wraps the flowers in cellophane and places them in a cooler. The flowers are packed 40 bunches in a box for shipment by air from Portland to any city in the U.S.

Back in the field, people are welcome to walk the rows of flowers with a catalog and choose what they would like to plant as bulbs in the fall. They may also buy flowers that will bloom in one to three days. The Iversons pass along helpful suggestions to their customers in person and through their catalog.

"We did surprisingly well this year," says Vicki Iverson. "The crop was good."

The Iversons have set aside 90 acres for rotating the tulips each year. With that and their ever-improving marketing strategies, including an overnight delivery package, the family's entrepreneurial zeal will keep their unique business in operation for many years to come — assuring a future for Ross and Dorothy's 18 grandchildren and future generations of Iversons.

Bernard Cleve and his son Robert on their ranch in Otero County, New Mexico. *Erik Ness, New Mexico Farm and Livestock Bureau*

A matched team, decked out in their best show harnesses brighten the Annual Mule Day in Columbia, Tenn.   *Pettus Read, Tennessee Farm Bureau Federation*

Chore time helper.   *Nellie Donovan, Pleasant View, Colo.*

Buckaroos, young and wise.   *Rick Bush, Florida Farm Bureau Federation*

Little Oregon cowboy Tyler McCormack and his grandfather Bill McCormack Sr.   *Stewart Truelsen, American Farm Bureau Federation*

Kentuckians visit the nation's Capitol. *Gary Huddleston, Kentucky Farm Bureau Federation*

Following page: Rick Treptow, Georgia Farm Bureau Federation

TAKING AGRICULTURE'S MESSAGE TO "THE HILL"

By Joan Waldoch
American Farm Bureau Federation

A group of Kentucky farmers gathered on a chilly spring morning in a Washington, D.C. hotel meeting room. These Farm Bureau members were not discussing the price of corn or the latest developments in dairy policy. They were listening to a discussion of the Endangered Species Act.

Their guest was of a species not likely to be headed for extinction — a Washington attorney who represented an activist environmental organization. The farmers listened and asked questions. When it was his turn to listen, the attorney nodded agreement when told that farmers, too, are environmentalists who care about the land.

The exchange is one illustration of how Farm Bureau groups broaden their lobbying efforts during visits to the nation's capital.

Washington visits are key to the organization's governmental relations program. Throughout the year, especially in the spring, thousands of Farm Bureau members travel to the capital, not as tourists, but as representatives of agriculture.

To a member of Congress, hearing directly from the folks back home is critical. Lawmakers benefit by hearing how issues affect constituents outside the beltway.

"They get insulated enough when they're in Congress," says Hyde Murray, an AFBF governmental relations director. "Having contact with constituents is a good reality check for them."

A lobbyist in Washington competes with tens of thousands of other advocates for the attention of government officials, making it difficult to establish direct contact. When groups of Farm Bureau members come to Washington, they provide valuable services in lobbying — access. Legislators' doors are opened for them.

"You can have the greatest trial lawyer in the world for a lobbyist, but if you can't get the ear of Congress that talent is not going to help you," says Murray.

For many Farm Bureau members, visiting Washington can be an eye-opener. Indiana farmer Donna Scanlon said meeting with members of Congress gave her a better understanding of the political process and agriculture's role in it. The agricultural population may be shrinking, but the number of issues that affect the industry definitely is not.

Washington visitors discover what busy schedules their lawmakers have. Between committee hearings and House or Senate floor votes, they — or their aides — meet with a steady stream of constituents representing all walks of life.

"They get pulled from so many directions," Scanlon said of lawmakers. "We in agriculture have to keep struggling to keep our voice heard."

While tourism is not the purpose of the Farm Bureau members' visits, they generally manage a few moments of sightseeing. No matter how much disenchantment people may feel toward our seat of government, they are impressed by the beauty of its architecture, monuments and historic sites.

"You read about these places and see them on television, but seeing them really brings it to life," said Scanlon. "You come back with a different perspective."

A rainy Kansas cattle drive.
John Schlageck, Kansas Farm Bureau

A lush, green Oregon valley. *Rick Stevenson, Oregon Farm Bureau Federation*

Orchard in bloom at the base of the California foothills.
California Farm Bureau Federation

Moving the sheep to greener pastures.
Linda Hamilton, Hyattville, Wyo.

Too pooped to root after entertaining children at farm day.   *Donna Hellwig Reynolds, Georgia Farm Bureau Federation*

The grass is always greener at Richard Byham's dairy farm. *Wilson Smeltz, Pennsylvania Farm Bureau*

Last battle before the boiling pot. *Michael Danna, Louisiana Farm Bureau Federation*

Following page: Michael Danna, Louisiana Farm Bureau Federation

FARM-FRESH CRAWFISH COMPLEMENT CAJUN CUISINE

By Michael Danna
Louisiana Farm Bureau Federation

They're sometimes referred to as "mudbugs." Crawfish farmers hate that. The fact is, there's nothing muddy, or dirty, about this Cajun delicacy, least of all to the farmers who make a living harvesting these clawed creatures from the ponds, swamps and bayous of South Louisiana.

Most Louisianans might say their crawfish originated in the Bayou State. We know better, but for the Cajuns it's fun to lay claim to a heritage foodstuff others use as fish bait.

Crawfish help put Louisiana on the culinary map, so to speak. Today, Louisiana crawfish (sometimes misspelled "crayfish") are shipped worldwide, from Sweden to Japan.

Wilbert Hebert, (pronounced A-bear), grew up with crawfish. As a retired rice farmer and native Cajun, the 70-year-old Hebert found that you can serve crawfish with rice. And even from the same field.

A flooded rice field is the perfect environment for raising crawfish. Following the harvest, rice stubble serves as excellent forage on which the crawfish dine.

Hebert, who has been a member of the Vermilion Parish Farm Bureau for 49 years, checks his crawfish traps twice a day in ponds near his home in Maurice, La. With son Dane, the two can be found in the early morning and late evening harvesting crawfish.

To check his traps, Hebert moves around his ponds in a modified aluminum boat, whose power system is a paddle wheel of sorts. The engine of the family's old riding lawn mower was resurrected and provides the power to turn the wheel. Rather than floating, the boat actually "rolls" across the shallow ponds.

When he was farming, Hebert said crawfish helped his cash flow between crops. It still serves as income. "It helps the farm cash flow during the winter months before the planting season," he said. "You can do the shop work part of the day and fish the rest. It gives you a little spending money so you don't have to borrow money during the winter."

Louisiana by far leads the nation in crawfish production. In 1991, nearly 60 million pounds of crawfish, worth about $35 million, was produced, the bulk of which was consumed at home.

Boiled with a liberal amount of any number of seasonings, and with everything from corn to potatoes thrown in, the crawfish are enjoyed all spring, from February, the beginning of the season, to around the end of June.

Eating crawfish is simple. Break off the tail, peel the tail shell and eat the spicy meat.

"Laissez les bon temps rouller!" (Translated: "Let the good times roll!")

Marion Todd examines a comb from one of his beehives.   *Cecil Yancy, Georgia Farm Bureau Federation*

Jill Kurtz smiles from behind an Arizona desert gold peach tree. *Andy G. Kurtz, Arizona Farm Bureau Federation*

A teacher loads seed at an Ag in the Classroom workshop.
Tina Henderson, Nebraska Farm Bureau Federation

Mel Runyan takes a break.
Erik Ness, New Mexico Farm and Livestock Bureau

Taking a breather after a long ride. *Rick Bush, Florida Farm Bureau Federation*

Keeping the system rolling along.   *Don Seabrook*, The Wenatchee (Wash.) World

Running cattle on Nevada's Owyhee Desert. *C. J. Hadley, Carson City, Nev.*

Following page: Laura Flood, Arizona Cattlemen's Association

THE LEGACY OF RANCHING IN THE GRAND CANYON STATE

By Jeff Davis
Arizona Farm Bureau Federation

From the mountain forests of northern Arizona to the Sonoran Desert in the south, Arizona ranchers are accustomed to working in adverse conditions — snow, dust or the intense heat of summer.

Cattle and sheep ranching is a family tradition. In Arizona, the typical rancher has been on the same ranch for 28 years and the average Arizona ranch family has been in the business for 70 years.

The Arizona cattle industry is 300 years old and today produces enough beef to feed the state's 3.6 million people, plus another million.

Though a large state, more than half of Arizona's land is owned by the federal government and 27 percent is owned by Native American tribes. Most ranchers graze livestock across a checkerboard of private, state and federal lands.

Arizona ranchers are stewards of that land and the environment. They give back to the land what they use — sometimes more. Watering sites built by ranchers have helped Arizona wildlife populations grow to record numbers. The average ranch in the state supports 152 deer, 88 elk, 37 antelope and one wild horse and burro.

Virginia Radial, president of the Coconino County Farm Bureau and Cattlegrowers, says more and more ranchers are adopting an approach to rangeland management called holistic resource management, which takes into account ecosystems, biological diversity and livestock production.

"I am interested in what the land is going to be like in 100 years," she says. "I won't be here but somebody will, and I would like for our legacy to be that we had the courage to be different and to improve the land."

Perhaps the philosophy of Arizona ranchers is best represented by the 107-year-old CO-Bar Ranch in Flagstaff, which has the following production goals: "To produce a flourishing, beautiful countryside, which has high biodiversity, abundant wildlife, clean air and clean water. To produce financial profit from livestock, recreation, wildlife, water, timber, minerals and land development. To provide educational opportunities for ourselves, our children, employees and communities…"

Arizona State Rep. Polly Rosenbaum looks over the wares at the Arizona Farm-City Festival. *Jeff Davis, Arizona Farm Bureau Federation*

Headquarters of the "Lonestar State's" finest. *Larry Binz, Texas Farm Bureau*

Farm Bureau membership has its rewards. *John Schlageck, Kansas Farm Bureau*

Youngsters get a feel for agriculture during School Days on the Farm at Mississippi State University.   *Meg King, Mississippi Farm Bureau Federation*

Telfair County, Ga. Farm Bureau President H. B. Barnes, Jr., teaches his grandson and other students about commodities at a local farm day.   *Donna Hellwig Reynolds, Georgia Farm Bureau Federation*

School children visited the Friendly Acres dairy farm as part of New York Farm Bureau's Ag Career Day.

Joel Sussman, New York Farm Bureau

The Great Flood of '93.   *Dave McClelland, Illinois Farm Bureau*

Following page: Southeastern drought. Kathy Epping, American Farm Bureau Federation

40

FARM BUREAU MOBILIZES
DURING DOUBLE DISASTERS

By Christopher Noun
American Farm Bureau Federation

The summer of 1993 will forever be remembered for the great Midwestern floods and Southeastern drought. Images of destruction and devastation dwell in the minds of those who lived in the path of the unforgiving high waters and the sweltering dry heat. Through news stories and photographs, images of hopelessness and despair are etched in the minds of even those who viewed the disasters from afar.

Mother Nature is uncontrollable and unpredictable. Who could have ever imagined natural disasters with such drastic consequences would strike America's farmers simultaneously.

Memories of ruin and waste left by the double disasters are easy to recall. Pictures of neighbors, whose property, crops and belongings were spared, lending hands to neighbors who were not as fortunate, almost pale in comparison to images of flooded fields, floating homes and wilted and dried crops.

Farm Bureau members gave new meaning to assistance and help. Delivering needed supplies, serving food, filling sandbags, patrolling swollen levees and working from sunup to sundown to protect a stranger's crop — farmers helped farmers.

From hay-lifts for livestock producers in the Southeast, whose feed crops had withered, to a catfish and hushpuppy fry in a St. Charles, Mo. parking lot to feed hungry volunteer flood-fighters and victims, Farm Bureau members answered the call.

In some examples, the assistance that was offered was more than flood and drought victims could use or handle.

"I got a call from a Farm Bureau in Washington state, seeing if we needed some hay," said Blake Roderick, manager of the Pike County (Ill.) Farm Bureau, a heavily flooded county. "They said they would send a whole trainload down, but we just couldn't get any trains in here. People were willing to help out any way they could."

In any case, offers and donations were gladly accepted and heartfelt by flood and drought victims alike. The American Farm Bureau Federation established a Disaster Relief Fund to aid stricken farmers. The fund became a clearinghouse for monetary donations from farmers, corporations and county and state Farm Bureaus across the nation. Notes of encouragement and sympathy accompanied donation checks from people who recalled their own recent setbacks from earthquakes, tornadoes and hurricanes.

The natural disasters of the summer of 1993 proved the strength and compassion of the Farm Bureau family.

"Farm Bureaus have done everything, from sending prayers to lending helping hands," said Jerry Rodhouse, a Pike County Farm Bureau member, during the height of the flood . "The only thing holding this thing together is the love of the people. We are going to do this."

The empathy and caring extended to flood and drought victims during these trying times must never be forgotten.

Supplies for flood victims.   *Joe Fields, American Farm Bureau Federation*

In the wake of destruction.   *Tom McCosky, American Farm Bureau Federation*

A youngster picks a juicy strawberry. *Connecticut Department of Economic Development*

SUMMER

"And what is so rare as a day in June?
Then, if ever, come perfect days;
Then Heaven tries earth if it be in tune,
And over it softly her warm ear lays . . "

James Russell Lowell

Flowers at farmers' market.
Jeff Burkhead, Kansas Farm Bureau

A farmers' market, the Alaskan way.   *Bob Franklin, Alaska Farmers and Stockgrowers Association*

Watson Dorn Farm, South Carolina.   *Larry Kemmerlin, South Carolina Farm Bureau*

Trees frame a sparkling New York dairy. *Joel Sussman, New York Farm Bureau*

A poi plantation is one facet of Hawaiian agriculture.   *Don Parrish, American Farm Bureau Federation*

Bird's eye view of rural Delaware.   *Delaware Department of Agriculture*

South Dakota sunflower field. *South Dakota Tourism*

Maine potato field in bloom.   *Mark James, Maine Farm Bureau Association*

A lonesome Kansas combine. *Mace Thornton, American Farm Bureau Federation*

Following page: John Schlageck, Kansas Farm Bureau

GATHERING THE GRAIN ON A LONG, HOT DAY

By John Schlageck
Kansas Farm Bureau

I t's 9 a.m. and the sun blazes down on a patchwork of golden grain that dots the High Plains near Seguin, Kan. Several days of warm, 20-mile-per-hour southerly winds have turned the wheat crop to its ripened edge.

On this late-June morning, a roar of combines signals the beginning of the wheat harvest. Cutting begins about this time each day and continues until midnight, or when grain becomes too moist or too tough to cut.

Fifteen-minute meal breaks are the only time off in a 14-hour workday. Although the days seem to last forever, technology has made life easy, compared to the dusty, itchy life of yesteryear, when farmers sat on open-air seats and ate dust while sweat ran down their faces.

Today's giant combines look more like tanks rolling through a war game. Wilfrid Reinert pilots one of the 12-ton machines as easily as the family car. His combine is complete with contoured seat, soundproof cab wrapped in tinted glass, air-conditioning and stereo. A digital computer monitors the entire operation. Equipped with dual brakes, power steering and automatic transmission, the combine moves through the field at speeds up to 5 miles per hour, depending on yield and field conditions. One machine can harvest 3,500 bushels of wheat on a good day.

"There's nothing like seeing wheat like this bunch up into the header and slow our machines to a crawl," Reinert says, breaking into a wide grin. "Yields like this make farming fun."

When the bin is full, Reinert signals for the grain cart. As the cart approaches, the unloading auger swings hydraulically 90 degrees and spews 250 bushels into an accompanying vehicle.

Harold Koster and his three sons work with Reinert to pool manpower and machinery. Koster keeps the combines and trucks running and makes sure the moisture of the wheat remains below 13.5 percent — the level considered acceptable at the grain elevator.

Farmers hate harvest days when weather changes and the sun ducks in and out of the clouds. On those days, they baby-sit the crop. They test a field here, then move to another down the road, hoping to find wheat dry enough to harvest. No wonder farmers have been known to curse the weather.

Koster gathers a few kernels of spilled grain and sticks it into his mouth. He looks out over his land, where the machines are moving through clouds of dust and chaff.

"You gotta take what's given you in this country," he says, chewing the wheat that's by now turned to gum. "Some years, what you receive is better than others."

A Kansas farmer takes risks that test the strength of his spirit. He faces harvest with the hope of bounty. He makes his peace with God and keeps that same peace with his neighbor. Faced with the annual trials of raising a wheat crop, this is the only way a Kansan can live with himself, or anybody else.

There is always one in the crowd. *Vic Saunders, Utah Farm Bureau Federation*

A youngster bellows with Bessie during "Cows on the Concourse" in Madison, Wis.
Tom Thieding, Wisconsin Farm Bureau Federation

A barn with a view. *Vickie Rappe, Iowa Farm Bureau Federation*

David and Ed Motz peel off another sheet of sod at their farm in Hamilton County, Ohio.

George Robey, Ohio Farm Bureau Federation

"You know, I can remember when…"   *Ken Kashian, Illinois Farm Bureau*

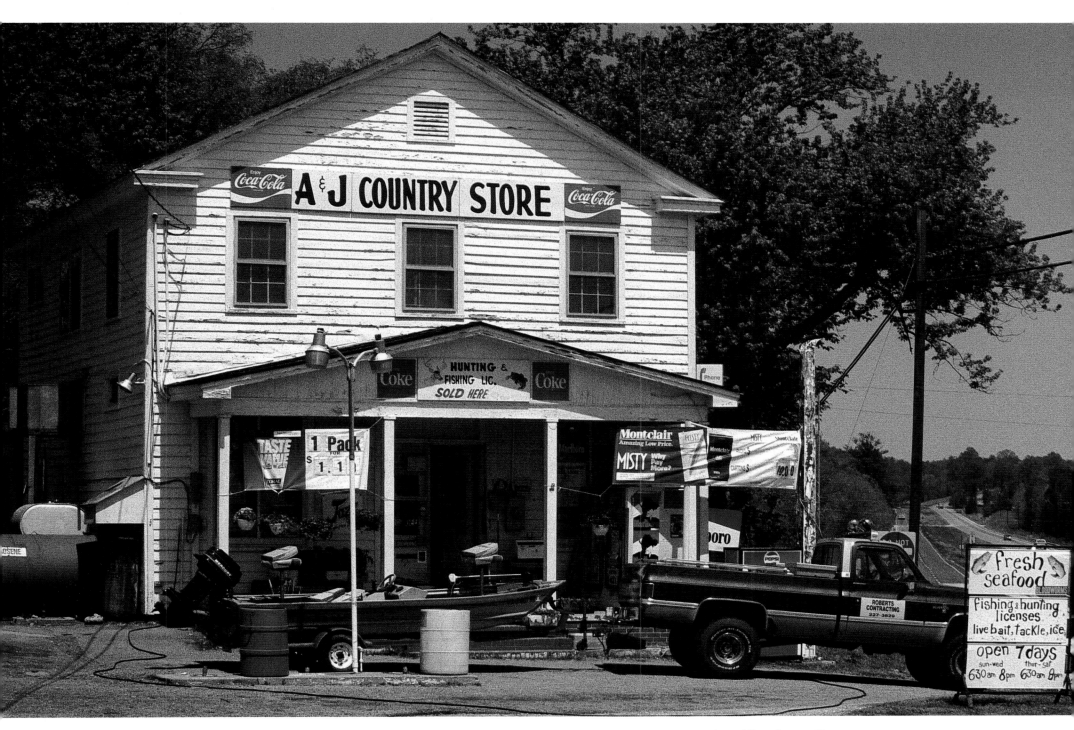

A roadside country store in King William County, Va. *Norm Hyde, Virginia Farm Bureau Federation*

Salem County, N. J. farmer Elmer Coles visits with New Jersey Farm
Bureau staffer Charlie Miller.   *New Jersey Farm Bureau*

Red, ripe Washington cherries just right for picking.
Don Seabrook, The Wenatchee (Wash.) World

Turkey-farming partners. *Don Seabrook*, The Wenatchee (Wash.) World

Chile peppers add spice to American agriculture.   *Erik Ness, New Mexico Farm and Livestock Bureau*

Following page: Erik Ness, New Mexico Farm and Livestock Bureau

AN ENCHANTED CROP IN AMERICA'S SOUTHWEST

By Erik Ness
New Mexico Farm & Livestock Bureau

A songwriter referred to New Mexico as "the land of red sunsets and green chile."

While New Mexico's motto is "Land of Enchantment," both lines paint an accurate image of the forty-seventh state — sometimes confused as a foreign country.

The state's proximity to the Republic of Mexico is one rivulet in a confluence of cultures that colorfully mixes the Old West with the terraced traditions of Native Americans, Hispanics and Anglos. Similarly, New Mexico's agricultural diversity ranges from beef and blue corn to pinto beans and peanuts, but perhaps no crop embodies the state's singular persona better than the ubiquitous chile pepper.

The most prevalent varieties — long red and green chile — have been bred to all degrees of heat and flavor and also seem to have developed an inherent public allure. The world is taking notice of the pungent peppers. Figures show Mexican cuisine is the fastest growing ethnic food segment in the United States, and salsa's popularity is rapidly gaining on ketchup's.

Dino Cervantes of Vado, N.M., is one of the new breed of chile farmers utilizing time-tested growing methods combined with the latest technology generated by researchers at New Mexico State University.

In his office is a desk piled with fresh, red and green chile and shelves stacked with products from across the nation — from Louisiana-style hot sauces to olives stuffed with jalapenos — that utilize his hot product. Take a bite and hang on.

The New Mexico chile crop relies on hand picking, but continuous governmental interference and red tape are pushing farmers toward mechanized picking. Like most farmers and ranchers, Cervantes says the "independence" of being a farmer is the No. 1 reason for his fast-paced career.

"Farming is a lot like sports," he points out. "You practice for three or four months out of the year, then you go to the big game and you win or lose. But then next year you can start over again."

Cervantes is active in his community and on the board of directors of the Dona Ana County Farm and Livestock Bureau. He says he joined Farm Bureau because it was a civic "responsibility." In addition, Cervantes notes that he gets "a lot of enjoyment out of it...it helps me grow intellectually and become more knowledgeable about issues affecting our community. Hopefully, somewhere down the road that will help me give something back."

The new generation of New Mexico farmers, like early Pueblo Indian agronomists, take great pride in their traditions and productive efforts. It's possible to find farms in New Mexico that have been in the same family since the 1500s, when Spanish Conquistadors brought their culture up the Rio Grande.

While the first agrarians in the Land of Enchantment worked hard all year to feed their own families, today's farmers work just as hard. The difference is they feed the entire world, and add a little heat on top, thanks to New Mexico's chile crop.

Finishing at the feedlot. *Don Seabrook,* The Wenatchee (Wash.) World

Teamwork on branding day. *Oklahoma Farm Bureau*

Travis Anderson's hand-fed North Dakota Longhorn.   *Joan Waldoch, American Farm Bureau Federation*

Colorful sunset near Chaffee, N.D. *Dawn Hvinden, North Dakota Farm Bureau*

The old swimming hole on Arkansas' Mulberry river.   *Jim Kester, Arkansas Farm Bureau Federation*

Keep your eye on the ball.   *Ken Kashian, Illinois Farm Bureau*

A young Michigan Farm Bureau patriot.   *Luke Schafer, Michigan Farm Bureau*

Eyes as big as a watermelon.   *Rick Bush, Florida Farm Bureau Federation*

Visitors register for Ag Progress Days in a Pennsylvania Farm Bureau
hospitality tent.   *Wilson Smeltz, Pennsylvania Farm Bureau*

Freddy Farm Bureau is a popular, annual attraction at the Kentucky State Fair.
Gary Huddleston, Kentucky Farm Bureau Federation

U. S. Senators Warner and Robb (Va.) visit Farm Bureau members in Washington, D.C.
Greg Hicks, Virginia Farm Bureau Federation

Farm Bureau at the Minnesota State Fair.   *Robin Kinney, Minnesota Farm Bureau Federation*

Alabama Farm Bureau's membership kickoff fish boil.
Robert C. Shepard, American Farm Bureau Federation

Showtime at the fair.   *Vermont Dept. of Travel and Tourism*

Getting into the swing of things at Young Farmer and Rancher Day at the North Carolina State Fair. *Don McCoy, North Carolina Farm Bureau Federation*

Colorful farmsteads mark Connecticut's rural
landscape.   *CT Department of Economic Development.*

Oregon farming is rich in tradition. *Rick Stevenson, Oregon Farm Bureau Federation*

American Farm Bureau Federation 75th Anniversary crop art.   *S. Cable Spence, American Farm Bureau Federation*

FALL

"O, it sets my heart a clickin' like the tickin' of a clock,
when the frost is on the punkin
and fodder's in the shock."

James Whitcomb Riley

A country road dressed in the hues of fall. *Ken Kashian, Illinois Farm Bureau*

California rice harvest. *California Farm Bureau Federation*

Pulling a wide load   *Don Seabrook*, The Wenatchee (Wash.) World

Harvesting a bumper crop.   *John Schlageck, Kansas Farm Bureau*

An old Farmall and young farmer Dan Hunsucker.   *Don McCoy, North Carolina Farm Bureau Federation*

Trimming the Christmas trees.   *Larry Kemmerlin, South Carolina Farm Bureau*

Pineapple harvest in Puerto Rico.   *Puerto Rico Department of Agriculture and San Juan, Puerto Rico Convention Bureau*

Cutting horse demonstration at the Sunbelt Ag Expo.   *Donna Hellwig Reynolds, Georgia Farm Bureau Federation*

A Florida tobacco farmer shows off his harvest.
Rick Bush, Florida Farm Bureau Federation

Sparks fly as a blacksmith puts hammer to anvil. *Rick Bush, Florida Farm Bureau Federation*

Lynn and Pamela Hawbaker carry on the tradition. *Ken Gordon, Indiana Farm Bureau*

Krystin and Justin Bachman enjoy apples, each in their own way.
Lynn Echelberger, Ohio Farm Bureau Federation

Farming is a family affair. *Larry Kemmerlin, South Carolina Farm Bureau*

Ripe cranberries on the vine.   *Bob Hawk, Northland Cranberries, Inc.*

Following page: Jeffrey LaFleur, Cape Cod Cranberry Growers' Association

HARVESTING AMERICA'S NATIVE FRUIT IN MASSACHUSETTS

By Pam Comstock
Massachusetts Farm Bureau

Wearing rubber waders and colorful flannel shirts, cranberry growers stand atop handmade "wet harvesting" machines. These mechanical mysteries crawl with almost imperceptible movement through the wet bog, gently agitating the vines to coax forth their crimson bounty.

Slowly, the water's surface reddens as berries bob to the top, freed from their bond with the vines. Up and down, back and forth the machines creep. Workers, deep in concentration, look straight down while every shade of red floats to the surface.

With the berries floating on the water, workers wade in, waist deep, to gently rake the fruit into floating wooden corrals, where it is sucked up a vacuum hose into a waiting box truck. From here, the fruit is on its way to many commercial markets.

A vast majority of the crop is wet harvested by first flooding the bogs. This accounts for virtually all of the fruit destined for juice drinks or as processed food. The beauty of wet harvest in southeastern Massachusetts, beneath a sunny, clear New England autumn landscape is a singular sight to behold. Watching the cranberry harvest is a major tourist attraction that frequently causes traffic jams on the interstate highways bordering cranberry bogs.

Only berries intended for fresh consumption are "dry harvested." Those pickers, resembling big, push lawn mowers, scoop the berries gently from their vines and sift them, minus their foliage, into an attached canvas bag. Picker bags are emptied into waiting bins and when full, the bins are lifted by helicopter onto flatbed trucks.

The first cranberries of the season become visible at the end of June or beginning of July. They reach deep, dark red maturity in mid-September — 80 days after full bloom. In southeastern Massachusetts, a large portion of the world's cranberry supply is grown and harvested on some 13,000 acres of bog. All told, cranberry growers in Massachusetts preserve more than 61,000 acres of upland, lowland and bog.

Cranberries are native to America, introduced to settlers by the earliest Americans in a variety of forms — as a sauce, a medicinal poultice and pounded into dried venison as pemmican.

The cultivated cranberry (Vaccinium macrocarpon) is a low-growing, trailing, woody broadleaf, non-deciduous vine. During the winter, leaves are reddish brown, turning dark, glossy green during the spring and summer growing season.

Thick vines form a matted cover over the surface of the cranberry beds producing stems or runners from one to six feet long, and from these, short, vertical, whorled, upright branches, two to three inches high. On these upright branches, the buds are formed, followed in mid-June by delicate, pink blossoms that last from three to six weeks.

The curve of the slender flower stem with the ready-to-open blossom is thought to resemble the neck and head of a crane, thus suggesting the origin of the name "cranberry," adapted from "craneberry."

Unloading corn keeps Brian and Liz Hirsch hopping on their farm.
Ken Gordon, Indiana Farm Bureau

Bountiful soybean harvest.   *John Schlageck, Kansas Farm Bureau*

Stacking Montana hay with a "Beaver slide."
Jules Marchesseault, Dillon, Mont.

Water trickles from an old windmill into a prairie stock tank.
Oklahoma Farm Bureau

Fall colors at Dells Pond and Mill in Eau Claire County, Wis.   *Paul Peterson, Wisconsin Farm Bureau Federation*

Bird hunting season in Western Kansas.
John Schlageck, Kansas Farm Bureau

Auburn waves of grain sorghum are about to be swallowed by an approaching combine.   *S. Cable Spence, American Farm Bureau Federation*

Purchasing fall's finest at "Holiday Harvest" in downtown St. Louis.
Chris Fennewald, Missouri Farm Bureau Federation

Pumpkins aplenty.   *Rhode Island Dept. of Economic Development*

Clouds roll over a Michigan farm. *Bonnie Zell, Lansing, Mich.*

An old-fashioned pig roast and get-together.
Minnesota Farm Bureau Federation

American farmers use the latest technology in decision-making. *Ken Kashian, Illinois Farm Bureau*

Another Farm Bureau service — insurance against life's calamities.
Ken Kashian, Illinois Farm Bureau

Alisa Sheridan learns about agriculture with the help of Ag in the Classroom Coordinator
Michelle Awad.   *Kathy Dixon, Virginia Farm Bureau Federation*

Harry Thompson demonstrates grain bin safety during Cole County, (Mo.) Farm
Bureau's "Operation Safety Shield".   *Mace Thornton, American Farm Bureau Federation*

U. S. Senator Dirk Kempthorne (Idaho) visits with schoolchildren during an Ag in the Classroom activity. *Mike Tracy, Idaho Farm Bureau Federation*

A barn peeks through snowy branches. *John Schlageck, Kansas Farm Bureau*

WINTER

"If we had no winter, the spring would not be so pleasant:
if we did not sometimes taste of adversity,
prosperity would not be so welcome."

Anne Bradstreet

Threshing rice the old-fashioned way.   *Kenneth Pettit, Corning, Ark.*

Winter snow blankets West Virginia barns.
Ross Straight, Buckhannon, W. Va.

A chilly moon hangs over an Indiana farmstead.
Ken Gordon, Indiana Farm Bureau

A Utah agricultural researcher chisels in ash to speed up snow melt. *Gary Neuenswander, Utah Agricultural Experiment Station*

The old country church still warms the ... Vermont Department of Travel and Tourism

Sugar pails hang heavy in late winter.   *Brenda Clemons, New Hampshire Farm Bureau*

Following page: Nancee Amey, Pittsburg, N. H.

SUGARING TIME IS A SWEET SEASON
IN NEW ENGLAND

By Brenda Clemons
New Hampshire Farm Bureau Federation

In New England there is a special time that comes before the whiteness of winter fades and spring unfolds. It is a season between seasons, when cool, crisp late winter nights awaken to the warmth of March sunshine, and the sap begins to flow in the maple grove.

Sugaring time, as New Englanders call it, brings long days of gathering and boiling that reach far into the night. The results are gratifying when the sweet sap transforms into smooth, delicious, golden maple syrup.

For the Amey family of Pittsburg, in the beautiful White Mountains of northern New Hampshire, a typical day means rising before dawn, tending to the dairy operation and then preparing for the two-mile trek to their "sugar camp" deep in the forest to begin their day of gathering and boiling.

The "sugar camp" is small with no electricity, just a wood stove, a small bunk bed and the essential equipment to make syrup. Hauling wood and most of the sap gathering from the 300-plus-tap sugar bush is done on foot. Sugaring time is definitely a family affair. John's wife, Nancy, his brother Mark, and the older Amey children all help.

After the wood is gathered and the sap collected, boiling begins. As night begins to fall and after a delicious lamb dinner made over the wood stove — a traditional menu item since the Ameys also raise sheep — Nancy and the children journey back to the farm. John and Mark stay on to finish the boiling, which will last until the early morning hours.

As the fire burns down, and the last bit of syrup is bottled, John and Mark close up the camp, strap on their snow shoes and make the trip back through the forest, prepared to do it all again the next day.

Within a few weeks the harvest is over, but the sweet taste of maple syrup will be savored throughout the year. The Amey family always celebrates the end of this special time of the year by inviting all the neighbors over for a "sugar on snow" party, complete with home-baked donuts and fresh apple cider.

A lone forager in a snowy corn field.   *Iowa Farm Bureau Federation*

Burning sugar cane prior to harvest.   *Rick Bush, Florida Farm Bureau Federation*

Draft horses pull a wintry load near Michigan's Mackinac Bridge.   *Mike Beaudoin, Mackinac Island Photography*

HORSES PULL THE LOAD ON MACKINAC ISLAND

By Connie Lawson
Michigan Farm Bureau

Even when Michigan's governor heads for Mackinac Island he is asked to leave his Oldsmobile on the peninsula. A long-standing prohibition against "horseless carriages" is still in effect. The governor is no exception.

Bill Chambers, veterinarian and an officer of the Mackinac Island Carriage Tours Company, says the ban has been on the books since 1897. Members of his family have run horse teams and carriages for five generations, serving the island economy, from fur trading and frontier outpost, to fishing and now tourism.

Less glamorous than the fancy carriages that grace summer weddings and parties on Mackinac Island, horse-drawn, winter freight wagons bring food and other supplies to the island's year-round residents and provide services such as garbage hauling.

The island's winter stable of 18 horses is just a small part of this company's horsepower. The Chamber's total herd of standard bred draft horses, Belgians, Percherons and Clydesdales numbers about 320.

Jim Chambers, Bill's brother, runs the Upper Peninsula farm and is president of Mackinac Island Carriage Tours. He is the acknowledged expert on horse care, management and training.

"My brother knows, raised or has bought every horse the company owns," Bill says. "He knows each animal right down to how it needs to be hitched and what side of the pole it works on."

Around the first weekend in May about 100 horses are brought to the island by ferry across the Straits of Mackinac from the home farm in Ste. Sault Marie. Light tourism in the early weeks of spring means light work for the animals, but as the weather warms and tourism increases, so does the size of the herd on the island.

By July, when the tourist season is in full swing, nearly 260 horses are needed to pull fancy wedding carriages, horse-drawn taxis, sight-seeing wagons and the supply wagons.

As Labor Day approaches, the fall pastures of the Chambers' farm await the animals, where over 1,100 acres in small parcels provide open land and grasses for the horses. Before October surrenders its fall color, most of the horses have been moved off the island by ferry. Back at the home farm for eight months of rest and relaxation, the horses are turned out to fall pasture.

But when Northern Michigan's bone-chilling winter arrives, the Chambers' farm becomes the horses' winter vacation resort. The winter stables are equipped in equine luxury — with barn shelter and stalls, and feedlot-exercise areas. The horses also are fed a special high calorie grain and hay diet to give fat protection from the freezing temperatures.

A helping hand on a snowy day.   *Don Seabrook,* The Wenatchee (Wash.) World

A chilly sip of water on the Montana range.   *Jules Marchesseault, Dillon, Mont.*

Winter snows sometimes bring extra feed for lucky sheep. *Linda Hamilton, Hyattville, Wyo.*

A handful of ferns from Hoblick Greens.   *Rick Bush, Florida Farm Bureau Federation*

Following page: Rick Bush, Florida Farm Bureau Federation

FERN FARMING IS
A DELICATE BUSINESS

By Rick Bush
Florida Farm Bureau Federation

With the sun still hours from rising, John Hoblick arrives at his office to begin the day. Its about 4 a.m. — his favorite time of the day. The office is quiet. No phones are ringing. And the ferns at Hoblick Greens lie under a blanket of fog, awaiting cutting crews that will soon arrive at the fernery near De Leon Springs on Florida's east coast.

John enjoys these quiet mornings, which become rarer as the weather cools and demand picks up for the dozen varieties of greens he provides to florists from New York to Denver. From Christmas to Mother's Day, John's schedule is filled with busy days and, often, sleepless nights.

Right in the middle of his busy season is Valentine's Day — the biggest day of the year for florists and fern growers. For weeks before the big day, John's crews cut ferns and ship them to wholesalers, where they will complement roses destined for sweethearts.

But when the season is at its peak, the weather seldom cooperates. Cold waves descend on Florida from the north, threatening the sensitive fern crop.

When a freeze is forecast, John spends days checking his irrigation pumps and sprinklers. The night of a freeze is too late to order more diesel fuel or replace sprinkler heads.

Through the night, as the temperature drops, John watches the thermometer. If he turns the sprinklers on at the right time, the water will coat the ferns in a layer of ice that holds the temperature at 32 degrees. If his timing is wrong, he risks losing his crop.

"This is a trendy industry," Hoblick says. From Christmas to June, he and several hundred other Florida fern growers stay busy harvesting the lush green fronds from about 7,000 acres of land in and around Volusia County.

Towering oaks provide the right amount of shade for delicate ferns that form an ankle-deep carpet across the land. At Hoblick Greens, John grows the leatherleaf fern — the staple of the industry — but by concentrating on special ferns like sprengeri, ming, nagi and coontie he has developed a special niche.

John's grandfather started Hoblick Greens in 1958. It was passed on to John's father, and John took over the business in 1990. He now manages production and cutting on the family's 28 acres and an additional 20 acres they manage. His wife, Kara, takes care of bookkeeping and filling orders.

Between growing ferns, dealing with customers, keeping up on water regulations, environmental laws and worker protection standards, John and Kara also take care of their three children.

Knowing the family name is on every box, John only packs and ships top quality ferns. The quality keeps buyers loyal.

Tending winter tomatoes in a Florida greenhouse.   *Rick Bush, Florida Farm Bureau Federation*

Extension agent Ralph Jordan leads a Delaware County, Ohio farm safety seminar.
Lynn Echelberger, Ohio Farm Bureau Federation

Wyoming sheep wait in line to be shorn.   *Linda Hamilton, Hyattville, Wyo.*

Twin calves and a helper.   *Teresa Harper, West Virginia Farm Bureau*

The Carlina and Dennis Harris Jr. family, New Mexico ranchers and
Farm Bureau members.   *Erik Ness, New Mexico Farm Bureau Livestock Bureau*

Molly McCoy takes her turn with the calf bottle. *Don McCoy, North Carolina Farm Bureau Federation*

Worth Cox, Carroll County, Va. Farm Bureau president, recruits Emmett Jones with the help of membership chairman Bernard Bowman. *Norm Hyde, Virginia Farm Bureau Federation*

Missouri farmers testify during a state property rights hearing.
Chris Fennewald, Missouri Farm Bureau Federation

FARM BUREAU: HISTORIC PAST... DYNAMIC FUTURE

Dean R. Kleckner, AFBF's 10th president

In 1919, a small group of farmers from a dozen states gathered in Chicago and founded the American Farm Bureau Federation. Their goal was to speak for themselves through their own national organization. Today, Farm Bureau is local, statewide, national and international in scope and influence.

The American Farm Bureau Federation is the world's largest voluntary organization of farmers and ranchers. More than 4 million families belong to county or parish Farm Bureaus, which, in turn, comprise state Farm Bureau organizations in all 50 states and Puerto Rico.

AFBF represents all commodity interests and is involved in all issues that are of concern to the nation's farmers and ranchers, from taxation to property rights. Farm Bureau is farm people joining together to solve common problems.

The organization has never been a government agency and it seeks support on a bipartisan basis. As the nation's largest farm organization, AFBF has established programs directed by policies that are developed and voted upon by farm representatives at the county, state and national levels.

Through the years, thousands of elected farm and ranch leaders have served on county and state Farm Bureau boards, with many serving as voting delegates in state and American Farm Bureau Federation business meetings. Just a few of these leaders — past and present state Farm Bureau presidents — are listed on the following pages (information provided by state Farm Bureaus). We salute this proud heritage as well as the foundation they have laid for future Farm Bureau leaders.

AMERICAN FARM BUREAU FEDERATION

Founded: November 12, 1919

Presidents	State	Term
J. R. Howard	Iowa	1920-1922
O. E. Bradfute	Ohio	1923-1925
Sam H. Thompson	Illinois	1926-1930
Edward A. O'Neal	Alabama	1931-1947
Allan B. Kline	Iowa	1948-1954
Charles B. Shuman	Illinois	1955-1970
William J. Kuhfuss	Illinois	1971-1975
Allan Grant	California	1976-1979
Robert B. Delano	Virginia	1980-1985
Dean R. Kleckner	Iowa	1986

American Farm Bureau Federation founding meeting, 1919.

ALABAMA FARM BUREAU FEDERATION
Founded: June 12, 1989

Presidents	Terms of Office
David McGriffe	1989-91
D. Delnor Denney	1991

ALASKA FARMERS AND STOCKGROWERS ASSN., INC.
Founded: December 1985

Presidents	Terms of Office
Jerry L. Giaugue	1986-1988
Terence W. Weiland	1988-1990
Robert "Bob" Franklin	1990

ARIZONA FARM BUREAU FEDERATION
Founded: 1921

Presidents	Terms of Office
C. S. (Farmer) Brown	1921-1924
*Information not available	1925-1935
Walter R. Strong	1936-1937
Hollis B. Gray	1938-1940
Nat M. Dysart	1940-1941
Cecil H. Miller Sr.	1941-1943
A. M. Ward	1943-1944
Clyde Neely	1945-1947
A. J. Fram	1948-1951
Floyd Hawkins	1951-1957
Jess C. Watt	1957-1958
Marvin R. Morrison	1958-1963
Floyd Hawkins	1963-1971
Cecil H. Miller Jr.	1971-1992
Ken Evans	1993

ARKANSAS FARM BUREAU FEDERATION
Founded: April 28, 1931

Presidents	Terms of Office
*Information not available	1931-1934
J. F. Thompkins	1935-1936
R. E. Short	1936-1948
Joe C. Hardin	1948-1955
Harold Ohlendorf	1955-1971
Morris Bowman	1971-1976
Nicky Hargrove	1976-1986
Andrew Whisenhunt	1986

CALIFORNIA FARM BUREAU FEDERATION
Founded: 1919

Presidents	Terms of Office
Dr. W. H. Walker	1919-1922
Dr. A. C. Hardison	1922-1925
Earl Houghton	1925-1927
A. Ahlf	1927-1929
R. W. Blackburn	1929-1938
Ray B. Wiser	1938-1951
George H. Wilson	1951-1955
Louis A. Rozzoni	1955-1963
Allan Grant	1963-1975
Frederick J. Heringer	1975-1981
Henry J. Voss	1981-1989
Bob L. Vice	1989

COLORADO FARM BUREAU
Founded: 1919

Presidents	Terms of Office
W. G. Jamison	1919
J. M. Rogers	1921
J. D. Pancake	1922
C. E. Gibson	1923-1925
*Information not available	1925-1928
B. F. Davis	1928-1930
J. C. Schecter	1931-1934
*Information not available	1935
A. Buettel	1936-1939
Ezra Alishouse	1940-1942
C. J. Phillips	1942-1946
Ezra Alishouse	1946-1952
A. L. Andersen	1953-1957
Lloyd Sommerville	1958-1973
T. Keith Propst	1974-1992
Roger Bill Mitchell	1993

CONNECTICUT FARM BUREAU ASSOCIATION, INC.
Founded: 1919

Presidents	Terms of Office
Theodore Savage	1919-1921
Dr. Walter C. Wood	1921-1925
S. McLean Buckingham	1925-1936
Samuel H. Graham	1936-1945
Edward P. Rowland	1945-1948

Frank W. Roberts	1948-1951
George C. Dudley	1951-1956
Rockwell W. Holcomb	1956-1960
Edward F. Dickau	1960-1963
Warren J. Foley	1963-1966
Luther Stearns	1966-1976
George Merrell	1976
Mary Porter	1976-1980
Luther Stearns	1980-1982
Norma O'Leary	1982

DELAWARE STATE FARM BUREAU, INC.
Founded: August 16, 1946

Presidents	Terms of Office
Floyd Short	1946-1952
George C. Simpson	1953-1954
James H. Baxter, Jr.	1954-1962
Roland E. Garrison	1962-1966
O. Joseph Penuel	1966- 1977
William L. David	1977
John F. Walton	1977-1982
John F. Tarburton	1982-1990
Joseph E. Calhoun	1991

FLORIDA FARM BUREAU FEDERATION
Founded: 1941

Presidents	Terms of Office
George I. Fullerton	1941-1942
John D. Clark	1942-1943
D. R. Igou	1943-1947
George W. Monroe	1947-1948
F. H. Corrigan	1948-1949
Loring Raoul	1949-1951
E. H. Finlayson	1951-1965
Arthur E. Karst	1965-1969
Walter J. Kautz	1969-1983
Carl B. Loop, Jr.	1983

GEORGIA FARM BUREAU FEDERATION

Founded: June 1937 as United Georgia Farmers
        April 1941 changed to Georgia Farm
        Bureau Federation

Presidents	Terms of Office
Robert M. Stiles	1937-1941
Harry L. Wingate	1941- 1957
John P. Duncan, Jr.	1957-1961
Dr. Harry L. Brown	1961-1964
William L. Lanier	1964-1970
W. J. McKemie, Jr.	1970
H. Emmett Reynolds	1970-1978
Robert L. Nash	1978-1988
T. M. "Mort" Ewing	1988

HAWAII FARM BUREAU FEDERATION

Founded: 1948

Presidents	Terms of Office
Masayuki Hanta	1948-1949
Kazuo Kikuta	1949-1951
Stanley Unten	1951-1952
Sam Tanna	1952-1953
Buddy Crabbe	1953-1954
Akira Sakima	1954-1956
Stanley Unten	1956-1957
Masaru Sumida	1957-1963
Phillip Shimabukuro	1963-1965
Wallace Nitta	1965-1977
Randall Kamiya	1978-1979
Dickie Nitta	1980-1982
Ron Terry	1982-1983
Sheridan Kobayashi	1983-1985
James Nakatani	1985

IDAHO FARM BUREAU FEDERATION

Founded: September 15, 1939

Presidents	Terms of Office
J. N. Dayley	1939-1945
George Yates	1946
A. W. Clegg	1947-1948
J. F. Frederickson	1949
J. Cyril Lau	1950
E. Duane Bingham	1951-1954
L. B. Martin	1955-1963

Nyal Rydalch	1964-1966
Monroe Hays	1967-1969
Dale Rockwood	1970-1973
Oscar Field	1973-1983
V. Thomas Geary	1984

ILLINOIS AGRICULTURAL ASSOCIATION

Founded: 1916

Presidents	Terms of Office
H. J. Sconce	1919
Howard Leonard	1920-1922
S. H. Thompson	1923-1926
Earl C. Smith	1927-1945
Charles B. Shuman	1946-1954
Otto Steffey	1955-1957
William J. Kuhfuss	1958-1970
Harold B. Steele	1971-1983
John White, Jr.	1984-1993
Alan Dale	1993

INDIANA FARM BUREAU, INC.

Founded: March 25, 1919

Presidents	Terms of Office
John G. Brown	1919-1922
William H. Settle	1923-1934
Lewis Taylor	1935-1936
Hassil E. Schenck	1936-1957
George Doup	1958-1976
Marion Stackhouse	1976-1987
Harry L. Pearson	1987

IOWA FARM BUREAU FEDERATION

Founded: December 27, 1918

Presidents	Terms of Office
J. R. Howard	1918-1920
C. W. Hunt	1921-1923
C. E. Hearst	1924-1935
Francis Johnson	1936-1943
Allan Kline	1944-1947
E. Howard Hill	1948-1963
J. Merrill Anderson	1963-1975
Dean R. Kleckner	1975-1986
Robert R. Joslin	1986-1987
Merlin D. Plagge	1987

KANSAS FARM BUREAU

Founded: October 21, 1919

Presidents	Terms of Office
Ralph Snyder	1919-1934
Dr. O. O. Wolf	1934-1944
Harold Harper	1944-1945
Herman Praeger	1945-1954
W. I. Boone	1954-1960
Walter C. Peirce	1960-1966
Ray Frisbie	1966-1972
John Junior Armstrong	1972-1983
Doyle D. Rahjes	1983

KENTUCKY FARM BUREAU FEDERATION

Founded: 1919

Presidents	Terms of Office
Gen. E. H. Woods	1919-1924
Harry Hartke	1925-1926
A. B. Sawyer, Jr.	1927-1930
J. C. Robinson	1931
J. E. Brown	1932
William Dempewolf	1932
C. G. Stephenson	1933-1934
O. C. Whitfield	1935
B. E. Niles	1936-1941
Rosco Stone	1941 (six months)
S. D. Broadbent	1942
A. H. Calvert	1943-1944
Lewis F. Allen	1945-1952
Burl S. St. Clair	1953-1962
Jack Welch	1963-1965
Louis F. Ison	1966-1973
J. Robert Wade	1974-1978
Ray Mackey	1979-1991
William R. Sprague	1992

LOUISIANA FARM BUREAU FEDERATION, INC.

Founded: 1921

Presidents	Terms of Office
J. H. Carpenter	1921-1922
A. L. Smith	1922-1924
Frank Dimmick	1924-1934
Wilmer C. Mills	1934-1936
H. G. Chalkley	1936-1943

Robert Amacker	1943-1944
Jim Percy	1944-1946
Malcom Dougherty	1946-1956
Larry L. Lovell	1956-1963
James D.Graugnard	1963-1989
Ronald R. Anderson	1989

MAINE FARM BUREAU ASSOCIATION
Founded: July 12, 1951

Presidents	Terms of Office
Frank W. Hussey	1951-1953
C. Wilder Smith	1953-1954
Rockwood N. Berry	1954-1958
Jerome Emerson	1958-1969
Benjamin Blackmore	1969-1976
Peter W. Curra	1976-1986
Dan LaPointe	1986

MARYLAND FARM BUREAU, INC.
Founded: June 1, 1916 as Maryland Agricultural
  Society

Presidents	Terms of Office
*Information not available	1916-1923
E. P. Cohill	1923-1926
James W. Davis	1926-1932
Charles T. Cockey	1933-1935
Harry H. Nuttle	1935-1939
Philip C. Turner	1939-1943
Roy C. F. Weagly	1943-1946
Howard S. Leaverton	1946-1949
Wilson A. Heaps	1949-1956
W.A. Cooksey	1956-1958
Randall S. Spoerlin	1958-1960
Noah Kefauver, Jr.	1960-1965
Y. D. Hance	1965-1967
Willard Oakley	1967-1972
T. Allan Stradley	1972-1974
F. Grove Miller	1974-1980
Leon Enfield	1980-1983
Henry Holloway	1983-1985
Robert E. Wilson	1985-1989
Edward J. Allen	1989-1991
C. William Knill	1991

MASSACHUSETTS FARM BUREAU FEDERATION, INC.
Founded: 1915

Presidents	Terms of Office
Horace A. Moses	1915
L. L. Richardson	1916
Evan Richardson	1917-1920
Harry Hinckley	1921-1922
Howard Russell	1923
John Chandler	1924
Leon Weatherbee	1925-1927
Raymond Dickinson	1928-1929
Elmer Poole	1930-1933
Robert P. Trask	1934-1935
Charlie Jordan	1936-1941
Joseph Decatur	1942-1945
Alfred G. Lunn	1946-1948
S. Lothrop Davenport	1948-1950
Lorenzo D. Lambson	1951-1952
Francis Barnard	1953-1959
Lloyd Hathaway	1960-1964
S. S. Garjian	1965-1967
Marshall Knowlton	1968-1971
David Mann	1972-1974
Harold Newton	1975-1980
Charles Dowse	1981-1987
A. Gordon Price	1988-1991
Richard D. Tryon	1992

MICHIGAN FARM BUREAU
Founded: 1919

Presidents	Terms of Office
Roland Morrill	1919-1921
James Nicol	1921-1923
Waldo E. Phillips	1923-1924
Michael L. Noon	1924-1926
Melville B. McPherson	1926-1927
Michael L. Noon	1927-1934
Watson W. Billings	1934-1935
Waldo E. Phillips	1935
James J. Jakway	1935-1939
Clarence J. Reid	1939-1945
Carl E. Buskirk	1945-1954

Ward G. Hodge	1954-1958
Walter W. Wightman	1958-1964
Elton R. Smith	1964-1986
John G. Laurie	1987

MINNESOTA FARM BUREAU FEDERATION
Founded: November 1919

Presidents	Terms of Office
V. E. Holmquist	1920
L. E. Potter	1920-1922
J. F. Reed	1922-1928
A. J. Olson	1928-1936
F. W. White	1936-1951
J. L. Morton	1951-1957
C. W. Myers	1957-1965
P. D. Hempstead	1965-1969
C. W. Wilson	1969-1977
M. W. Lokensgard	1977-1988
Al Christopherson	1988

MISSISSIPPI FARM BUREAU FEDERATION
Founded: October 1922

Presidents	Terms of Office
C. L. Neill	1922-1929
G. H. Alford	1929-1931
D. E. Wilson	1931-1937
Ransom Aldrich	1937-1950
Boswell Stevens	1950-1972
Hugh M. Arant	1973-1988
Don Waller	1989

MISSOURI FARM BUREAU FEDERATION

Founded: 1915

Presidents	Terms of Office
Dr. E. H. Bullock	1915-1917
H. G. Windsor	1917-1918
Chester Gray	1918-1922
John Boland	1922-1923
Charles Barron	1923-1924
L. M. Monsees	1924-1925
R. W. Brown	1925-1944
H. E. Slusher	1944-1958
Olen Monsees	1958-1966
Paul Pippitt	1966-1968
C. R. Johnston	1968-1988
Donald Fischer	1988-1992
Charles E. Kruse	1992

MONTANA FARM BUREAU FEDERATION

Founded: 1919

Presidents	Terms of Office
John M. Davis	1919-1920
W. B. Harland	1920-1922
A. H. Stafford	1922-1924
W. L. Stockton	1924-1930
W. S. McCormack	1930-1933
Norman L. Towne	1933-1939
Claude C. Gray	1939-1947
Clarkson Spain	1947-1953
George Diehl	1953-1959
Max P. Maberry	1959-1961
Henry F. Wilson	1961-1967
Bernard Harkness	1967-1980
T. M. "Mack" Quinn	1980-1985
Gene Chapel	1985-1986
Donald Ochsner	1986-1987
David L. McClure	1987

NEBRASKA FARM BUREAU FEDERATION

Founded: 1917

Presidents	Terms of Office
Harry Keefe	1917-1918
Elmer Young	1918-1922
J. N. Norton	1922
C. Y. Thompson	1922-1923
Harry Keefe	1923-1925
Nellie Benson	1925-1929
L. R. Leonard	1929-1930
Charles H. Murray	1930-1931
P. P. Ceder	1931-1933
C. Y. Thompson	1933-1945
Charles Marshall	1945-1966
Roland Nelson	1966-1972
John Klinker	1972-1975
Wendell Gangwish	1975-1981
Bryce P. Neidig	1981

NEVADA FARM BUREAU FEDERATION

Founded: 1919   Incorporated: 1920

Presidents	Terms of Office
E. C. Riddell	1920-1921
W. A. Hardy	1923-1924
J. D. Yeager	1925-1934
George F. Ogilvie	1935-1942
*Information not available	1943-1955
James Sharp	1956-1962
Norman Glaser	1962-1963
Robert Thomas	1963-1968
Andrew N. Hanson	1969-1970
Norman T. Shurtliff	1970-1972
M. Jeoffry Dahl	1973-1977
Tim Hafen	1977-1981
Dave Fulstone ll	1981-1988
Barbara Curti	1988

NEW HAMPSHIRE FARM BUREAU FEDERATION

Founded: December 15, 1916

Presidents	Terms of Office
Roy D. Hunter	1916-1917
George M. Putnam	1917-1950
George A. Bassett	1950-1954
Stacey Cole	1954-1961
Richard G. Kelley	1961-1962
A. Paul Stimson	1962-1965
G. Allen Holmes	1965-1975
Lawrence Underhill	1975-1980
Errol Peters	1980-1986
Sheldon S. Sawyer	1986-1991
Gordon H. Gowen	1991

NEW JERSEY FARM BUREAU

Founded: October 6, 1919

Presidents	Terms of Office
Harry E. Taylor	1919-1924
Howard B. Hancock	1925-1927
William C. Spargo	1928-1934
Dr. Frank App	1934-1941
Herbert W. Voorhees	1942-1959
Carleton E. Heritage	1959-1966
Arthur H. West	1967-1980
T. Lauren DeCou	1980-1982
Walter Ellis, Jr.	1982-1988
Stephen J. George	1988

NEW MEXICO FARM & LIVESTOCK BUREAU

Founded: May 1, 1917

Presidents	Terms of Office
James R. Poe	before1930
L .E. Frudenthal	1930-1937
A. W. Hockenhull	1937-1938
A. H. Gerdeman	1938-1940
G. D. Hatfield	1940-1942
W. P. Thorpe	1942-1946
Delmar Roberts	1946-1956
W. B. McAlister	1956-1962
A. W. Langenegger	1962-1978
L. E. "Pete" Davis	1978-1984
William E. McIlhaney	1985-1992
John Van Sweden	1993

NEW YORK FARM BUREAU, INC.

Founded: February 17, 1917

Presidents	Terms of Office
S. L. Strivings	1917-1922
Enos Lee	1923-1925
Peter Ten Eyck	1926
C. R. White	1927-1933
George Lamb	1934
Herbert King	1935-1940
Chester DuMond	1941-1942
Warren Hawley	1943-1954
Don Wickham	1954-1958
Don Green	1959-1961

William Bensley	1961-1968
Robert Greig	1968-1970
Richard McGuire	1970-1984
Phil Griffen	1984-1985
Charles E. Wille	1985

NORTH CAROLINA FARM BUREAU FEDERATION, INC.
Founded: April 1, 1936

Presidents	Terms of Office
J.E. Winslow	1936-1946
W. W. "Cap" Eagles	1946-1949
A. C. "Lon" Edwards	1949-1951
P. N. Taylor	1951-1953
C. Gordon Maddrey	1953-1954
A. D. Williams	1954-1956
W. Randolph Eagles	1956-1959
B. C. Mangum	1959-1974
John W. Sledge	1974-1985
W. B. "Bob" Jenkins	1985

NORTH DAKOTA FARM BUREAU
Founded: 1942

Presidents	Terms of Office
W. A. Plath	1942-1949
P. J. Donnelly	1949-1957
G. H. Mikkelson	1957-1958
R. D. Magill	1958-1959
G. H. Mikkelson	1959-1962
Clark Robinson	1962-1968
Ken McIntyre	1968-1969
Harold Langseth	1969-1972
Francis Sinner	1972-1979
Robert Kadrmas	1979-1982
Monty Burke	1982-1990
Howard Schmid	1990

OHIO FARM BUREAU FEDERATION, INC.
Founded: 1919

Presidents	Terms of Office
O. E. Bradfute	1919-1922
L. B. Palmer	1923-1933
Perry L. Green	1934-1948
Robert Peelle	1948-1949

Everett F. Rittenour	1949-1954
H. D. Heckathorn	1954-1959
Ferris Owen	1959-1960
Wendell Weller	1960-1965
Frank Sollars	1965-1968
Robert Summer	1968-1972
Leonard Schnell	1972-1975
Wallace Hirschfeld	1975-1981
David O. Miller	1981-1985
James Patterson	1985-1989
Fred Finney	1989-1992
C. Ray Noecker	1992

OKLAHOMA FARM BUREAU
Founded: March 4, 1942

Presidents	Terms of Office
John I. Taylor	1942-1953
Lewis H. Munn	1953-1975
Billy Jarvis	1975-1977
James L. Lockett	1977

OREGON FARM BUREAU FEDERATION
Founded: 1932

Presidents	Terms of Office
Mac Hoke	1935-1945
Lowell Steen	1945-1950
Marshal Swearingen	1950-1953
Ben Robinson	1953-1955
Gerald Detering	1955-1961
Wiley Clowers	1961-1962
Harold Beach	1962-1965
Claude Williams	1965-1969
Ralph Robinson	1969-1973
Waldron Johnson	1973-1979
Frank Setniker	1979-1983
Robert W. Hukari	1983-1987
Douglas H. Breese	1987

PENNSYLVANIA FARMERS' ASSOCIATION (PENN. FARM BUREAU)
Founded: 1950

Presidents	Terms of Office
T. P. Kirby	1950-1953
G. A. Biggs	1953-1969

John R. Pitzer	1969-1976
Eugene Thompson	1976-1981
Keith W. Eckel	1981

PUERTO RICO FARM BUREAU
Founded:1924

Presidents	Terms of Office
Rafael ma. Gonzalez	1924-1930
Jose Pesquera	1930-1934
Carlos Blondet	1935-1936
Antonio R. Matos	1937
Jose Pesquera	1938
Miguel Martorell	1939-1944
Jose R. Quinones	1945-1954
Oreste Ramos	1955-1973
Luis R. Berrios	1974-1979
Luis A. Becerra	1980-1983
Luis Torres	1984-1987
Antonio Alvarez	1987-1990
Moraima Rivera	1990-1992
Fernando Toledo	1992

RHODE ISLAND FARM BUREAU FEDERATION, INC.
Founded: November 30, 1952

Presidents	Terms of Office
Burton Froberg	1952-1956
Grover J. Douglas	1956-1958
Everett I. Cornell, Jr.	1959
Mervin C. Briggs	1959-1962
William Morgan, Jr.	1962-1974
William M. Stamp, Jr.	1974

SOUTH CAROLINA FARM BUREAU
Founded: April 19,1944

Presidents	Terms of Office
Robert R. Coker	1944-1945
E. H. Agnew	1945-1961
David H. Sloan, Jr.	1961-1971
Harry S. Bell	1971

SOUTH DAKOTA FARM BUREAU FEDERATION

Founded: 1917

Presidents	Terms of Office
Herbert C. Cobb	1917-1921
William S. Hill	1921-1923
Willis H. Davis	1923-1926
Robert M. Crowder	1926-1929
Howard B. Test	1929-1945
Edward A. Johnson	1945-1951
Albert Keffeler	1951-1955
John Foster	1955-1963
Tom McNenny	1963-1967
Henry Knochenmus	1967-1975
Richard Ekstrum	1975

TENNESSEE FARM BUREAU FEDERATION

Founded: July 1921

Presidents	Terms of Office
Joe F. Porter	1921-1946
Tom Hitch	1947-1961
Clyde M. York	1962-1973
James Putman	1974-1986
Joe Hawkins	1987

TEXAS FARM BUREAU

Founded:1933

Presidents	Terms of Office
J. Walter Hammond	1939-1957
J. H. West	1957-1962
C. H. DeVaney	1962-1967
Sidney Dean	1967-1970
J. T. Woodson	1970-1974
Carrol Chaloupka	1974-1982
S. M. True, Jr.	1982

UTAH FARM BUREAU FEDERATION

Founded: December 4, 1916

Presidents	Terms of Office
D. D. McKay	1916-1921
Ephraim Bergeson	1921-1926
M. B. Brown	1926-1927
David Beal	1927-1928
Ephraim Bergeson	1928-1931
George Stallings	1931-1933
Joseph Anderson	1933-1937
Ward Holbrook	1937-1942
George Hobson	1942-1948

Alden Barton	1948-1950
John Schenk	1950-1954
Blaine Swenson	1954-1955
A. V. Smoot	1955-1966
Elmo Hamilton	1966-1977
Frank Nishiguchi	1977-1986
Kenneth R. Ashby	1986

VERMONT FARM BUREAU, INC.

Founded: 1915

Presidents	Terms of Office
Ellsworth B. Cornwall	1919-1928
Arthur H. Packard	1928-1953
Keith Wallace	1953-1974
Rupert C. Chamberlain	1974-1986
Walter F. Pyle	1986

VIRGINIA FARM BUREAU FEDERATION

Founded: 1921

Presidents	Terms of Office
Governor Henry Carter Stuart	early '20's
Captain D. H. Barger	until 1928
Gabriel F. Holsinger	1928-1947
Howard S. Zigler	1947-1948
H. Guy Blalock	1948-1956
Roy B. Davis, Jr.	1956-1958
T. T. Curtis	1958-1962
Robert B. Delano	1962-1980
S. T. Moore, Jr.	1980-1986
Robert B. Delano	1986-1988
C. Wayne Ashworth	1988

WASHINGTON STATE FARM BUREAU FEDERATION

Founded: November 1921

Presidents	Terms of Office
*Information not available	1921-1945
Ralph Gillespie	1945-1957
Heber Thompson	1957-1960
Max Benitz	1960-1968
Melvin Ammerman	1968-1972
Ray DeVries	1972-1974
Robert Stuhmiller	1974-1978
Herb Strueli	1978-1979
Robert Jones	1979-1988
Darrell O. Turner	1988

WEST VIRGINIA FARM BUREAU FEDERATION, INC.

Founded: 1919

Presidents	Terms of Office
A. C. Huff	1918
J. B. McLaughlin	1919
W. D. Zinn	1920-1921
J. W. Carskaden	1922-1923
C.A. Jackson	1924
W. P. Ireland	1925-1926
E. S. Humphrey	1927-1934
John M. Bailey	1935-1940
Clyde Bonar	1941-1954
Raymond Balenger	1955-1960
Paul Nay	1961-1983
Fred G. Butler	1984

WISCONSIN FARM BUREAU FEDERATION

Founded: May 27, 1920

Presidents	Terms of Office
George W. Hull	1920-1921
George McKerrow	1921-1924
George W. Hull	1924-1925
Orrin S. Fletcher	1925-1926
Hugh A. Harper	1926-1927
W. G. Patterson	1927-1928
Fred E. Coldren	1928-1930
Hugh C. Hemmingway	1930-1932
Joseph W. Schwartz	1932-1940
Hugh C. Hemmingway	1940-1942
Roscoe Smith	1942-1943
Curtis Hatch	1943-1958
Percy S. Hardiman	1959-1969
Neelian O. Nelson	1969-1971
Donald R. Haldeman	1971-1991
Howard D. Poulson	1991

WYOMING FARM BUREAU FEDERATION

Founded: 1920

Presidents	Terms of Office
John Gonin	1920-1921
Dwight O. Herrick	1921
H. J. King	1923-1948
Kleber H. Hadsell	1949
Reuben V. Anderson	1950-1960
Herbert D. Livingston	1960-1970
David A. Flitner	1970